The Philosophy of Nature

Georg Hegel

Table of Contents

The Philosophy of Nature

Georg Hegel

Preliminary Concepts

§ 192.

Nature has presented itself as the idea in the form of otherness.

Since in nature the idea is as the negative of itself or is external to itself nature is not merely external in relation to this idea, but the externality constitutes the determination in which nature as nature exists.

§ 193.

In this externality the determinations of the concept have the appearance of an indifferent subsistence and isolation in regards to each other. The concept therefore exists as an inward entity. Hence nature exhibits no freedom in its existence, but only necessity and contingency.

For this reason nature, in the determinate existence, which makes it nature, is not to be deified, nor are the sun, moon, animals, plants, and so on, to be regarded and adduced as the works of God, more excellent than human actions and events. Nature in itself in the idea, is divine, but in the specific mode by which it is nature it is suspended. As it is, the being of nature does not correspond to its concept; its existing actuality therefore has no truth; its abstract essence is the negative, as the ancients conceived of matter in general as the non–ens. But because, even in this element, nature is a representation of the idea, one may very well admire in it the wisdom of God. If however, as Vanini said, a stalk of straw suffices to demonstrate God's being, then every representation of the spirit, the slightest fancy of the mind, the play of its most capricious whim, every word, offers a ground for the knowledge of God's being that is superior to any single object of nature. In nature, not only is the play of forms unbound and unchecked in contingency, but each figure for itself lacks the concept of itself. The highest level to which nature drives its existence is life, but as only a natural idea this is at the mercy of the unreason of externality, and individual vitality is in each moment of its existence entangled with an individuality which is other to it, whereas in every expression of the spirit is contained the moment of free, universal self–relation. – Nature in general is justly determined as the decline of the idea from itself because in the element of externality it has the determination of the inappropriateness of itself with itself.–A similar misunderstanding is to regard human works of art as inferior to natural things, on the grounds that works of art must take their material from outside, and that they are not alive.–It is as if the spiritual form did not contain a higher level of life, and were not more worthy of the spirit than the natural form, and as if in all ethical things what can be called matter did not belong solely to the spirit –

Nature remains, despite all the contingency of its existence, obedient to eternal laws; but surely this is also true of the realm of selfconsciousness, a fact which can already be seen in the belief that providence governs human affairs. Or are the determinations of this providence in the field of human affairs only contingent and irrational? But if the contingency of spirit, the free will, leads to evil, is this not still infinitely higher than the regular behaviour of the stars, or the innocence of the plants?

§ 194.

Nature is to be viewed as a system of stages, in which one stage necessarily arises from the other and is the truth closest to the other from which it results, though not in such a way that the one would naturally generate the other, but rather in the inner idea which constitutes the ground of nature.

It has been an awkward conception in older and also more recent philosophy of nature to see the progression and the transition of one natural form and sphere into another as an external, actual production which, however, in order to be made clearer, is relegated to the darkness of the past. Precisely this externality is characteristic of nature: differences are allowed to fall apart and to appear as existences indifferent to each other; and the dialectical concept, which leads the stages further, is the interior which emerges only in the spirit. Certainly the previously favoured teleological view provided the basis for the relation to the concept, and, in the same way, the relation to the spirit, but it focused only on external purposiveness–(cf § 151) and viewed the spirit as if it were entangled in finite and natural purposes. Due to the vapidity of such finite purposes, purposes for which natural things were shown to be useful, the teleological view has been discredited for exhibiting the wisdom of God. The view of the usefulness of natural things has the implicit truth that these things are not in and for themselves an absolute goal; nevertheless, it is unable to determine whether such things are defective or inadequate. For this determination it is necessary to posit that the immanent moment of its idea, which brings about its transiency and transition into another existence, produces at the same time a transformation into a higher concept.

§ 195.

Nature is, in itself a living whole. The movement of its idea through its sequence of stages is more precisely this: the idea posits itself as that which it is in itself; or, what is the same thing, it goes into itself out of that immediacy and externality which is death in order to go into itself; yet further, it suspends this determinacy of the idea, in which it is only life, and becomes spirit, which is its truth.

§ 196.

The idea as nature is: (1) as universal, ideal being outside of itself space and time; (2) as real and mutual being apart from itself particular or material existence, – inorganic nature; (3) as living actuality, organic nature. The three sciences can thus be named mathematics, physics, and physiology.

I. Mathematics

§ 197.

(1) The first or immediate determination of nature is the abstract generality of its self–externality,–its unmediated indifference, space. It is the wholly ideal juxtaposition, because it is being outside of itself and absolutely continuous, because this being apart from itself is still entirely abstract, and has no specific difference within itself.

Much has been said, from different theoretical positions, about the nature of space. I will mention only the Kantian determination that space is, like time, a form of sensory intuition. It has also become customary to establish fundamentally that space must be regarded only as something subjective in representation. Disregarding what, in the Kantian conception, belongs to subjective idealism and its determinations (cf § 5), the correct determination remains that space is a mere form, i.e., an abstraction, that of immediate externality. – To speak of points of space, as if they constituted the positive element of space, is inadmissible, since space, on account of its lack of differentiation, is only the possibility and not the positing of that which is negative and therefore absolutely continuous. The point is therefore rather the negation of space.–This also settles the question of the infinitude of space. Space is in general pure quantity (§ 53f), though no longer as a logical determination, but rather as existing immediately and externally. Nature, consequently, does not begin with quality but with quantity, because its determination is not, like logical being, the absolute first and immediate, but essentially a mediated being, a being external to and other than itself

§ 198.

Space has, as the concept in general (and more determinate than an indifferent self–externality) its differences within it: (a) in its indifference these are immediately the three dimensions, which are merely diverse and quite indeterminate.

But geometry is not required to deduce that space necessarily has precisely three dimensions, for it is not a philosophical science, and may therefore presuppose space as its object. Moreover, even apart from this, no thought is given to the demonstration of such a necessity. The necessity rests on the nature of the concept, whose determinations, however, because they depict themselves in these first elements of being apart from themselves, in abstract quantity, are only entirely superficial and a completely empty difference. One can also, therefore, not say how height, length, and width differ from each other, because they only ought to be different, but are not yet differences.–Height has its more precise determination as direction according to the center of the earth, but this does not at all concern the nature of space for itself Following from this point it is equally as indifferent whether this direction is called height or depth, or length or breadth, which is also often called depth.

§ 199.

(b) But the difference of space is essentially a determinate, qualitative difference. As such it is (a) first, the negation of space itself because this is immediate and undifferentiated self–externality, the point. (b) The negation as negation, however, is itself spatial, and the relation of the point to space is the line, the first otherness of the point. (c) The truth of the otherness is, however, the negation of the negation. The line, therefore, passes over into the plane, which on the one hand is a determinacy opposed to line and point, and thus is plane in general, but on the other hand is the suspended negation of space, and thus the re–establishment of spatial totality, which, however, now contains the negative moment within itself an enclosing surface, which splits off an individual, whole space.

That the line does not consist of points, nor the plane of lines, follows from their concepts, for the line is the point existing outside of itself relating itself to space, and suspending itself and the plane is just as much the suspended line existing outside of itself.–Here the point is represented as the first and positive entity, and taken as the starting point. The converse, though, is also true: in as far as space is positive, the plane is the first negation and the line is the second, which, however, is in its truth the negation relating self to self the point. The necessity of the transition is the same.–

The other configurations of space considered by geometry are further qualitative limitations of a spatial abstraction, of the plane, or of a limited spatial whole. Here there occur a few necessary moments, for example, that the triangle is the first rectilinear figure, that all other figures must, to be determined, be reduced to it or to the square, and so on.–The principle of these figures is the identity of the understanding, which determines the figurations as regular, and in this way grounds the relationships and sets them in place, which it now becomes the purpose of science to know.

It may be noted in passing that it was an extraordinary notion of Kant's to claim that the definition of the straight line as the shortest distance between two points is a synthetic proposition, for my concept of straightness contains nothing of size, but only a quality. In this sense every definition is a synthetic proposition. What is defined, the straight line, is in the first place the intuition or representation, and the determination that it is the shortest distance between two points constitutes in the first place the concept (namely, as it appears in such definitions, cf. § 110). That the concept is not already given by the intuition constitutes precisely the difference between the two, and is what calls for a definition. That something seems to the representation to be a quality, though its specificity rests on a quantitative determination, is something very simple, and also the case for example with the right angle, the straight line, and so on.

§ 200.

(2) Negativity, which as point relates itself to space and in space develops its determinations as line and plane, is, however, in the sphere of self–externality equally for itself and appearing indifferent to the motionless coexistence of space. Negativity, thus posited for itself is time.

§ 201.

Time, as the negative unity of being outside of itself, is just as thoroughly abstract, ideal being: being which, since it is, is not, and since it is not, is.

Tune, like space, is a pure form of sensuousness, or intuition; but, as with space, the difference between objectivity and a contrastingly subjective consciousness does not matter to time. If these determinations are applied to space and time, then space is abstract objectivity, whereas time is abstract subjectivity. Time is the same principle as the I = I of pure self–consciousness; but the same principle or the simple concept still in its entire externality, intuited mere becoming, pure being in itself as sheer coming out of itself. Time is just as continuous as space, for it is abstract negativity relating itself to itself and in this abstraction there is as yet no real difference.

In time, it is said, everything arises and passes away, or rather, there appears precisely the abstraction of arising and falling away. If abstractions are made from everything, namely, from the fullness of time just as much as from the fullness of space, then there remains both empty time and empty space left over; that is, there are then posited these abstractions of exteriority.–But time itself is this becoming, this existing abstraction, the Chronos who gives birth to everything and destroys his offspring.–That which is real, however, is just as identical to as distinct from time. Everything is transitory that is temporal, that is, exists only in time or, like the concept, is not in itself pure negativity. To be sure, this negativity is in everything as its immanent, universal essence, but the temporal is not adequate to this essence, and therefore relates to this negativity in terms of its power. Time itself is eternal, for it is neither just any time, nor the moment now, but time as time is its concept. The concept, however, in its identity with itself I= 1, is in and for itself absolute negativity and freedom. Time, is not, therefore, the power of the concept, nor is the concept in time and temporal; on the contrary, the concept is the power of time, which is only this negativity as externality.–The natural is therefore subordinate to time, insofar as it is finite; that which is true, by contrast, the idea, the spirit, is eternal. Thus the concept of eternity must not be grasped as if it were suspended time, or in any case not in the sense that eternity would come after time, for this would turn eternity into the future, in other words into a moment of time. And the concept of eternity must also not be understood in the sense of a negation of time, so that it would be merely an abstraction of time. For time in its concept is, like the concept itself generally, eternal, and therefore also absolute presence.

§ 202.

The dimensions of time, the present, future, and past, are only that which is becoming and its dissolution into the differences of being as the transition into nothingness, and of Nothingness as the transition into being. The immediate disappearance of these differences into individuality is the present as now, which is itself only this disappearance of being into nothingness, and of nothingness into being.

(1) The finite present is differentiated from the infinite in that the finite is the moment now and hence as its abstract moments, as past and future, which is different from the infinite as from the concrete unity. Eternity as concept, h r, contains these moments in itself and its concrete unity is therefore not the moment now, because it is motionless identity, concrete being as universal, and not that which is disappearing into nothingness, as becoming.–Furthermore in nature, where time is now, there does not occur the subsisting difference of these dimensions; they are necessarily only in subjective representation, in memory, fear, or hope. The abstract past, however, and future of time is

space, as the suspended space is at first the point and time.

(2) There is no science of time in opposition to the finite science of space, geometry, because the differences of time do not have the indifference of being outside of itself which constitutes the immediate determinacy of space, and therefore they can not be expressed as spatial configurations. The principle of time only reaches this ability when the understanding has paralysed it and reduced its negativity to the unit. This motionless unit, as the sheer carnality of thought, can be used to form external combinations, and these, the numbers of arithmetic, can themselves be brought under the categories of the truth as intuition or as understanding merely for itself because the latter is only abstract, whereas the former is concrete. This dead unit, now the highest externality of thought, can be used to form external combinations, and these combinations, the figures of arithmetic, can in turn be organised by the determination of the understanding in terms of equality and inequality, identity and difference. The science which has unity as its principle is therefore constituted in opposition to geometry.

(3) The name of mathematics has moreover been used for the philosophical observation of space and time, because it lies close to this observation, despite the fact that mathematics, as noted, considers strictly the determinations of magnitude of its objects and not time itself but only the unit in its configurations and connections. To be sure, time becomes in the theory of movement an object of science, but applied mathematics is generally not an immanent science, precisely because it involves the application of pure mathematics to a given material and its determinations as derived from experience.

(4) One could still, however, conceive the thought of a philosophical mathematics, namely, as a science which would recognise those concepts which constitute what the conventional mathematical science of the understanding derives from its presupposed determinations, and according to the method of the understanding, without concepts. However, since mathematics is the science of the finite determinations of magnitude, which remain fixed in their finitude and valid, and should not change in transit, thus it is essentially a science of the understanding. And since it has the ability to express spatial figures and numbers, which gives it an advantage over other sciences of this kind, it ought to retain this ability for itself and to avoid contamination by either concepts, like time, which are heterogeneous to it, or empirical purposes. It therefore remains open for the concept to establish a more fundamental consciousness than has hitherto been shown, both in terms of the leading principles of the understanding and in terms of order and its

necessity in arithmetical operations, as well as in the theses of geometry.–If one wanted to treat the forms of space and the unit philosophically, they would lose on these grounds their particular significance, a philosophy of them would become a matter of logic, or would even assume the character of another concrete philosophical science, according to the ways one imparted a more concrete significance to the concepts.–

It would, however, be a superfluous and thankless task to try to use such an unmanageable and inadequate medium as spatial figures and numbers for the expression of thoughts, and to treat them violently for this purpose. For the specific concept would always be related only externally to them. The simple elementary figures and numbers can in any case be used as symbols, which, however, are a subordinate and poor expression for thoughts. The first attempts of pure thought took recourse to such aids: the Pythagorean system of numbers is the famous example of this. But with richer concepts these means became completely unsatisfactory, since their external juxtaposition and contingent combination are not at all appropriate to the nature of the concept, and make it altogether ambiguous which of the many possible relationships in complex numbers and figures should be adhered to. Besides, the fluid character of the concept is dissipated in such an external medium, in which each determination falls into the indifferent being outside the others. This ambiguity could only be removed by an explanation. The essential expression of the thought is in that case this explanation, and this symbolising is an empty superfluity.

Other mathematical determinations, such as infinity and its relationships, the infinitesimal, factors, powers, and so ' on, have their true concepts in philosophy itself. It is awkward to want to take and derive these from mathematics, where they are employed in a nonconceptual, often meaningless way; rather, they must await their justification and significance from philosophy. The truly philosophical science of mathematics as theory of magnitude would be the science of measures, but this already presupposes the real particularity of things, which is only at hand in concrete nature.

§ 203.

(5) Space and time constitute the idea in and for itself, with space the real or immediately objective side and time the purely subjective side. Space is in itself the contradiction of indifferent being outside of others and undifferentiated continuity, and thereby the pure negativity of itself and the transition into time. Space converts into the individuality of

the place. Time is, equally, since its moments held together in unity suspend themselves immediately, the immediate convergence into indifference, into undifferentiated being apart from one another, or into space, so that its place is precisely in that way immediate as sheer indifferent spatiality. This disappearance and regeneration of space in time and of time in space is motion;–a becoming, which, however, is itself just as much immediately the identically existing unity of both, or matter.

The transition from ideality to reality, from abstraction to concrete existence, in this case from space and time to reality, which appears as matter, is incomprehensible to the understanding, and always converts therefore externally for the understanding, and as a given entity. The usual conception is to take space and time as empty and to be filled with matter from the outside. In this way material things are, on the one hand, to be taken as indifferent to space and time, and on the other hand to be taken at the same time as essentially spatial and temporal.

What is usually said of matter is: (a) that it is composite; this refers to its identity with space. Insofar as abstractions are made from time and from all form generally, it is asserted that matter is eternal and immutable. In fact, this follows immediately, but such a matter is also only an untrue abstraction. (b) It is said that matter is impenetrable and offers resistance, is tangible, visible, and so on. These predicates mean nothing else than that matter exists, partly for specific forms of perception, in general for an other, but partly just as much for itself Both of these are determinations which belong to matter precisely because it is the identity of space and time, of immediate being apart from itself or of becoming.

The transition of ideality into reality is demonstrated therefore in the familiar mechanical phenomena, namely, that ideality can take the place of reality and vice versa; and only the usual thoughtlessness of the representation and of the understanding are to blame that, for them, their identity does not derive from the interchangeability of both. In connection with the lever, for example, distance can be posited in the place of mass and vice versa, and a quantum of the ideal moment produces the same effect as the corresponding real moment.

Similarly, velocity, in the magnitude of motion, the quantitative relationship of space and time, represents mass, and conversely, the same real effect emerges if the mass is increased and the velocity proportionately decreased. By itself a brick does not kill a person, but produces this effect only though the velocity it achieves, in other words, the person is killed through space and time.

It is force, a category of reflection fixed by the understanding, which presents itself here as the ultimate, and therefore prevents understanding and lets it seem superfluous to inquire further after the concept. But this at least appears without thought, namely, that the effect of force is something real and appealing to the senses, and in force there is realised that which is in its expression; indeed, it appears that force achieves precisely this force of its expression through the relationship of its ideal moments, of space and time.

Further, it is also in keeping with this nonconceptual reflection that "forces' are seen as implanted in matter, and as originally external to it, so that this very identity of time–and space, which vaguely appears in the reflective category of force, and which in truth constitutes the essence of matter, is posited as something alien to it and contingent, something introduced into it from outside.

II. Inorganic Physics

A. Mechanics – B. Elementary Physics – C. The Physics of Individuality

§ 204.

Matter in itself holds itself apart from itself through the moment of its negativity, diversity, or abstract separation into parts; it has repulsion. Its being apart from itself is just as essential, however, because these differences are one and the same: the negative unity of this existence apart from itself as being for itself, and thus continuous. Matter therefore has attraction. The unity of these moments is gravity.

Kant has, among other things, through the attempt at a "construction" of matter in his metaphysical elements of the natural sciences, the merit of having started towards a concept of matter, after it had been attributed merely to the deadness of the understanding and its determinations had been conceived as the relations of attributes. With this attempt Kant revived the concept of the philosophy of nature, which is nothing other than the comprehension of nature or, what is the same, the knowledge of the concept in nature.

But in so doing he assumed that the reflective categories of attraction and repulsion were readymade, and further, he presupposed that the category of the reflection itself out of which matter should emerge, is readymade. This confusion is a necessary consequence of Kant's procedure, because the former abstract moments can not be conceptualised without their identity; moreover, because the observation of these opposing determinations suspends itself immediately in their identity, there is the danger that they will appear, like attraction, as a mere continuity. I have demonstrated in detail the confusion which dominates Kant's exposition in my system of Logic, vol. 1, part 1, pp. 119ff.

§ 205.

Matter, as having gravity, is only: (1) matter existing in itself or general. But this concept must: (2) specify itself; thus it is elementary matter, and the object of elementary physics. (3) Particular matter taken together is individualised matter, and the object of physics as the actual world of the body.

A. Mechanics

§ 206.

Matter, as simply general, has at first only a quantitative difference, and particularises itself into different quanta, – masses, which, in the superficial determination of a whole or one, are bodies.

§ 207.

The body is: (1) as heavy matter the solid identity of space and time, but (2) as the first negation it has in itself their ideality, which differentiates them from each other and from the body. The body is essentially in space and time, of which it constitutes its indifferent content in contrast to this form.

§ 208.

(3) As space, in which time is suspended, the body is enduring, and (4) as time, in which the indifferent subsistence of space is suspended, the body is transitory. In general, it is a

wholly contingent unit. (5) But as the unity which binds together the two moments in their opposition, the body essentially has motion, and the appearance of gravity.

Because the forces have been seen as only implanted onto matter, motion in particular is considered to be a determination external to the body, even by that physics which is presumably scientific. It has thus become a leading axiom of mechanics that the body is set in motion or placed into a condition only by an external cause. On the one hand it is the understanding which holds motion and rest apart as nonconceptual determinations, and therefore does not grasp their transition into each other, but on the other hand only the selfless bodies of the earth,. which are the object of ordinary mechanics, appear in this representation. The determinations, which occur in the appearance of such bodies and are valid, are set as the foundation, and the nature of the independent bodies is subsumed under this category. In fact, however, the latter are truly more general and the former is that which is subsumed absolutely, and in absolute mechanics the concept presents itself in its truth and singularity.

§ 209.

In motion, time posits itself spatially as place, but this indifferent spatiality becomes just as immediately temporal: the place becomes another (cf § 202). This difference of time and space is, as the difference of their absolute unity and their indifferent content, a difference of bodies, which hold themselves apart from each other yet equally seek their unity through gravity; — general gravitation.

§ 210.

Gravitation is the true and determinate concept of material corporeality, which is thereby just as essentially divided into particular bodies, and which has its manifested existence, the moment of external individuality, in movement, which is thus determined immediately as a relation of several bodies.

General gravitation must be recognised for itself as a profound thought, which constitutes an absolute basis for mechanics if it is conceived initially in the sphere of reflection, though it is so bound up with it through the quantitative determinations that it has attracted attention and credit, and its verification has been based solely on the experience analysed from the solar system down to the phenomenon of the capillary tubes. Certainly gravitation directly contradicts the law of inertia, for, by virtue of the former, matter strives to get out of itself to another. In the concept of gravity, as has been shown, there are included the two moments of being for itself and of that continuity that suspends being for itself These moments of the concept now experience the fate, as particular forces corresponding to the power of attraction and repulsion, of being conceived more precisely as the centripetal and the centrifugal forces, which are supposed, like gravity, to act on bodies, and independently of each other and contingently, to meet together in a third entity, the body. In this way whatever profundity was contained in the thought of general gravitation is destroyed again, and the concept and reason will be unable to penetrate into the theory of absolute motion, as long as the vaunted discoveries of forces prevail there.

if one closely considers the quantitative determinations which have been identified in the laws of the centripetal and the centrifugal forces, one very quickly discovers the confusion which emerges from their separation. This confusion becomes even greater if the separation is mentioned in relation to gravitation; gravitation, also called attraction, then seems to be the same as centripetal force, the law of this individual force is taken as the law of the whole of gravitation, and the centrifugal force, which at another time is valued as thoroughly essential, is viewed as something quite superfluous.–In the above proposition, which contains the immediate idea of gravitation, gravity itself namely, as the concept, which shows itself in the particularity of the body through the external reality of motion, the rational identity and inseparability of these two moments are contained.–The relativity of motion also shows itself in this proposition, which only makes sense in a system of several bodies standing in relation to each other in accordance with a varied determination, so that a different determination will immediately result.

§ 211.

The particular bodies in which gravity is realised have, as the determinations of their different natures, the moments of their concept. One body, therefore, is the general centre of being in itself. Opposing this extreme stands individuality, existing outside of itself and without a centre. But the particular bodies are others, which stand in the determination of being outside of themselves and are at the same time, as being in themselves, also centres for themselves, and are related to the first body as to their essential unity.

§ 212.

(1) The motion of bodies of relative centrality, in relation to bodies of abstract, general centrality, is absolutely free motion, and the conclusion of this system is that the general central body is brought together through relative centrality with dependent corporeality.

As is well–known, the laws of absolutely free motion were discovered by Kepler, a discovery of immortal fame. Kepler proved them, too, in the sense that he found the general expression for the empirical data (cf § 145). Since then it has become a commonplace that Newton first found the proofs of these laws. Not often has fame been more unjustly transferred from the first discoverer to another. Here I only want to point out what has basically already been admitted by mathematicians, namely: (1) that the Newtonian formulas can be derived from Keplerian laws; (2) that the Newtonian proof of the proposition that a body governed by the law of gravitation moves in an ellipse around the central body proceeds in general in a conic section, whereas the main point that was to be proven consists precisely in this, that the course of such a body is neither a circle nor any other conic section, but solely the ellipse. The conditions which make the course of the body into a specific conic section are referred back to an empirical condition, namely, a particular situation of the body at a specific point in time, and to the contingent strength of an impulse which it is supposed to have received at the beginning. (3) Newton's 'law" of the force of gravity has likewise only been demonstrated inductively from experience.

On closer inspection it appears that what Kepler, in a simple and sublime manner, articulated in the form of laws of celestial motion, Newton converted into the nonconceptual, reflective form of the force of gravity. The whole manner of this "proof" presents in general a confused tissue of lines of merely geometrical construction to which a physical meaning of independent forces is given, of the empty concepts of the understanding of a force of acceleration, of particles of time, at whose beginning those forces always play a renewed role, and of a force of inertia, which presumably continues its previous effect, and so on. A rational proof of the quantitative determinations of free motion can only rest on the determinations of the concepts of space and time, the moments whose relation is motion.

§ 213.

(2) The absolute relation of those dependent bodies, which are merely the extreme of the being outside of itself of gravity and therefore lack their own centrality to their relative central bodies, is the residual element of their gravity in them, which because of physical being outside of themselves is mere striving and, therefore, a pressure directed towards the centre lying outside of them.

§ 214.

The separation of the immediate connection in which such a body rests is a contingent condition, which the body, if confronted with an external impediment, suspends as motion, – relatively free motion in which the distancing from the body is not attributed as dependent, but the motion, if the impediment is removed, is immanent to the body and a manifestation of its own gravity. This motion transforms itself for itself into rest.

The attractive force of the sun, for example towards the planets, or of the earth towards those independent bodies belonging to it, seems to suggest the skewed view that the force would be an activity inhabiting the central body, and that the bodies found in its sphere would behave only passively and externally. Thus absolute motion is also viewed, through the application of terms from common mechanics, as the dead conflict of an independent, tangential force and of a force deriving equally independently from the middle point, from which the body would be passively drawn.

The Galilean law of falling, namely, that traversed spaces behave as the squares of transpired times, shows, in contrast to the abstract, homogeneous velocity of the lifeless mechanism, where spaces are proportional to times, the liberation of the conceptual determinations of time and space. In these terms the former has the determination of the root as the negative moment or principle of one, whereas the latter has the determination of the square as a being outside of itself more specifically, without another determinacy like that of the root, a coming outside of itself. In this law both moments still remain in the relation, because the freedom of motion in falling, which is also conditioned, is only formal. By contrast, in absolute motion there is the relation in its totality, since this is the realm of free measures in which each determinacy attains its totality. Because the law is essentially relational, time and space are retained in their original difference. Dimensionless time achieves therefore only a formal identity with itself; space, on the other hand, as positive being outside of itself achieves the dimension of the concept. The Keplerian law is thus the relation of the cubes of the distances to the squares of the times;–a law which is so great because it simply and directly depicts the reason of the thing. The Newtonian formula, however, which transforms it into a law for the force of gravity, exhibits only the perversion and inversion of reflection which has stopped halfway.

§ 215.

(3) In the extremity of dependent bodies, general gravitation, which bodies have as matter toward each other, is subordinated to the gravitation which they have towards their shared central bodies. Towards each other, then, their motion is external and contingent; the cause of the motion is thrust and pressure. In this common mechanical motion the size of the mass, which has no meaning in the fall, and the resistance, which the size achieves through its particular constitution, are moments of determination. But because this motion contradicts the essential relation of the dependent body, namely, that relation to its central body, it suspends itself through itself in rest. This necessity of the concept appears, however, in the sphere of externality, as an external impediment or friction.

The law of inertia is initially taken from the nature of the motion of dependent bodies, for which the motion, because it involves the difference from themselves for themselves, is external. But precisely for this reason rest is immanent to the bodies, namely, the identity with the centre lying outside of them. Their motion converts therefore essentially into rest, but not into absolute rest, rather into the pressure of striving towards their centre. This centre, if it is to be seen as a striving moment, is at the least the transformation of that external movement into the striving which constitutes the nature of the body.

The individual impediment, or the general one, the friction, is external, to be sure, but also necessary. It is the manifestation of that transition posited by the concept of the dependent body. And precisely this can also be found in consideration of the pendulum, the motion of which, it is said, would continue without stopping if friction could be removed.

For itself the law of inertia expresses nothing but the fixation of the understanding on the abstractions of rest and motion, which state that rest is only rest and motion is only motion. The transformation of these abstractions into each other, which is the concept, is for the understanding something external. This law of inertia, together with thrust, attraction, and other determinations have been inadmissibly transposed from common mechanics into absolute mechanics, where motion is rather to be found in its free concept.

§ 216.

The difference between central and dependent bodies is in the implicit being of gravity, whose identical nature is its existence. The dependent body has the beginning of the real difference as the being outside of itself of the gravity identical to itself; the dependent body has only a negative centre and therefore can only move around the centre simply as mass. The determinacy of its motion is not in and for itself but refers back to a factor which is the mass of the other, so that their sizes can be exchanged, and the motion remains the same.

§ 217.

This externality of determinate being constitutes the special determinacy of matter. But in this it does not remain limited by a quantitative difference, rather the difference is essentially a qualitative one, so that the determinacy of matter constitutes its being.

The empty abstraction of formless matter contains a merely quantitative difference and views its further determinacy as a form inessential to it. Even the forces of attraction and repulsion are supposed to influence it externally. Since it is the concept positing itself outside of itself it is so identical to the specific form that the form constitutes its special nature.

B. Elementary Physics

§ 218.

Gravity, as the essence of matter existing in itself only inner identity, transforms, since its concept is the essential externality, into the manifestation of the essence. As such it is the totality of the determinations of reflection, but these as thrown apart from each other, so that each appears as particular, qualified matter which, not yet determined as individuality, is a formless element.

The determination of an element is the being for itself of matter as it finds its point of unity in the concept, though this does not yet have to do with the determination of a physical element, which is still real matter, a totality of its qualities existing in itself.

(a) Elementary Particles

§ 219.

(1) Matter in its first elementary state is pure identity, not inwardly, but as existing, that is, the relation to itself determined as independent in contrast to the other determinations of totality. This existing self of matter is light.

§ 220.

As the abstract self of matter, light is absolutely lightweight, and as matter, infinite, but as material ideality it is inseparable and simple being outside of itself.

In the Oriental intuition of the substantial unity of the spiritual and the natural, the pure selfhood of consciousness, thought identical with itself as the abstraction of the true and the good is one with light. When the conception which has been called realistic denies that ideality is present in nature, it need only be referred to light, to that pure manifestation which is nothing but manifestation.

Heavy matter is divisible into masses, since it is concrete identity and quantity; but in the highly abstract ideality of light there is no such distinction; a limitation of light in its infinite expansion does not suspend its absolute connection. The conception of discrete, simple, rays of light, and of particles and bundles of them which are supposed to constitute light in its limited expansion, belongs among the rest of the conceptual barbarism which has, particularly since Newton, become dominant in physics. The indivisibility of light in its infinite expansion, a reality outside of itself that remains self–identical, can least of all be treated as incomprehensible by the understanding, for its own principle is rather this abstract identity.

Astronomers have come to speak of celestial phenomena which are perceived by us five hundred years and more after their actual occurrence. In this one can see, on the one hand, empirical manifestations of the propagation of light, carried over from a sphere where they obtain into another where they have no meaning, but on the other hand a past which has become present in ideal fashion as in memory.

There is also the conception of light which suggests that from each point of a visible surface beams are emitted in every direction, so that from each point a material hemisphere of infinite dimensions is formed, and that all of these infinitely many hemispheres interpenetrate each other. If this were so a dense, confused mass should form between the eye and the object, and the still–unexplained visibility would rather, on the basis of this explanation, give way to invisibility. The whole conception reduces to an absurdity, somewhat like the conception of a concrete body which is presumed to consist of many substances, with each existing in the pores of the other, in which, conversely, the others exist and circulate. Through this comprehensive penetration the assumption of the discrete materiality of the supposedly real substances is destroyed, and an entirely ideal relationship is established.

The self–like nature of light, insofar as it vitalises natural things, individualises them, and strengthens and holds together their unfolding, first becomes manifest in the individualisation of matter, for the initially abstract identity is only as return and suspension of particularity the negative unity of individuality.

§ 221.

Light behaves as a general identity, initially in this determination of diversity, or the determination by the understanding of the moment of totality, then to concrete matter as an external and other entity, as to darkening. This contact and external darkening of the one by the other is colour.

According to the familiar Newtonian theory, white, or colourless light consists of five or seven colours; – the theory itself can not say exactly how many. One can not express oneself strongly enough about the barbarism, in the first place, of the conception that with light, too, the worst form of reflection, the compound, was seized upon, so that brightness here could consist of seven darknesses, or water could consist of seven forms of earth. Further, the ineptitude, tastelessness, even dishonesty of Newton's observations and experimentations must be addressed, as well as the equally bad tendency to draw inferences, conclusions, and proofs from impure empirical data. Moreover, the blindness of the admiration given to Newton's work for nearly one and a half centuries must be noted, the narrowmindedness of those admirers who defend his conceptions, and, in particular, the thoughtlessness with which a number of the immediate conclusions of that theory (for example, the impossibility of an achromatic telescope) were dropped, although the theory itself is still maintained. Finally, there is the blindness of the prejudice that the theory rests on something mathematical, as if the partly false and one–sided measurements, as well as the quantitative determinations brought into the conclusions, would provide any basis for the theory and the nature of the thing itself.–A major reason why the clear, thorough, and learned illumination by Goethe of this darkness concerning light has not had a more effective reception is doubtlessly because the thoughtlessness and simplemindedness, which one would have to confess for following Newton for so long, would be entirely too great.

Instead of these nonsensical conceptions disappearing, they have recently been compounded by the discoveries of Malus, by the idea of a polarisation of light, the notion of the four–sidedness of sunbeams, and the idea that red beams rotate in a movement to the left, whereas blue beams rotate in a movement to the right. Such simplistic ideas seem justified by the privilege accorded to physics to generate "hypotheses." But even as a joke one does not indulge in stupidities; thus so much the less should stupidities be offered as hypotheses which are not even meant to be jokes.

§ 222.

Light shapes the determinate being or the physical meaning of the body of abstract centrality in the determination of its identity. Light is the active identity which posits everything as identical. As this identity, however, is still wholly abstract, things are not yet really identical, but are for an other, positing their identity with the other in the other.

§ 223.

This abstract identity has its real antithesis outside of itself. As an elementary moment of reflection it falls apart into itself and is as a duality: (a) of corporeal diversity, of material being for itself of rigidity; (b) of opposition as such, which, existing independently and uncontrolled by individuality, has merely sunken within itself and is thus dissolution and neutrality. The former is the lunar, the latter is the cometary body.

As relative central bodies in the system of gravity these two bodies have their more specific significance, which is based on the same concept as their physical significance and may be stated here: they do not rotate on their axes. The body of rigidity has only a formal being for itself which is independence comprehended in antithesis and therefore not individuality. Hence it is subservient to another body whose satellite it is, and in which it has its axis. The body of dissolution, on the other hand, the opposite of the body of rigidity, behaves aberrantly, and exhibits contingency in its eccentric path as in its physical existence. One can therefore suspect of these bodies that the proximity of a large planet could change their course. They show themselves to be a superficial concretion, which may just contingently turn itself again into dust.

The moon has no atmosphere and therefore lacks the meteorological process. It shows only high mountains and craters, and the combustion of this rigidity in itself It has the shape of a crystal, which Heim (one of the few ingenious geologists) has described as the original form of the earth as a merely solid body.

The comet appears as a formal process and unstable mass of vapour; none of them has exhibited anything of a solid nature, such as a nucleus. In contrast to the image of the ancients, that comets are merely meteors, more recent astronomers have not been as inflexible and presumptuous. Until now only the return of some of them has been demonstrated; others were calculated to return, but did not arrive. Suggestions brought forward by astronomers also indicate that the previously held formal view of comets, as crisscross manifestations appearing in conflict with the coherence of the system, should in time be discarded. Then the idea could be accepted that the other bodies of the system protect themselves against comets, that is, that the other bodies of the system function as necessary organic moments of protection. This view would afford better grounds for comfort in regards to the dangers of comets than the reasons which have been adduced so far.

§ 224.

(3) The antithesis that has gone back into itself is the earth or the planet as such. It is the body of the individual totality, in which rigidity opens up into a separation of real differences, and this dissolution is held together by self–like points of unity.

One is accustomed to seeing the sun and the stars as more excellent natures than the planets, because the first elevation of the reflection above sensory perception sets the abstract as the highest point against that individual element which is not yet conceptualised. The name of a "mad star" has arisen for individual bodies from the immediate view of their motion. In and for itself however, this motion of the individual bodies as a turning on an axis around itself and also around a central body is the most concrete expression of vitality, and therefore more splendid than both the stillness in the centre of the system, and the subservient and extravagant motion of the lunar and cometary bodies. The natural light of the central body is equally its abstract identity, with its truth, like that of thought, in the concrete idea, in individuality.

In regards to the series of planets, astronomy has still not discovered any actual law governing the determination of their proximity, their distancing, or even anything rational–I no longer find satisfying what I tried to show in an earlier dissertation about this issue.–Moreover, the attempts by the philosophy of nature to demonstrate the rationality of the series in its physical constitution, which have until now been merely preliminary attempts to establish basic perspectives, can also be viewed as unsatisfactory. What is irrational is to establish the thought of contingency as the basis, and to see the idea of the organisation of the solar system according to the laws of musical harmony, as for example in Kepler's thought, as an imaginative confusion, and not to respect the profound belief that

there is reason in this system. For this belief was the sole basis of Kepler's discoveries. Instead, it was the wholly awkward and confused use of the numerical relations of tones, applied by Newton to colours, which acquired fame and remembrance.

(b.) The Elements

§ 225.

The body of individuality contains the determinations of elemental totality, which have an immediate existence as free, independent bodies, as subordinate moments. As such they constitute general physical elements.

§ 226.

(1) The element of undifferentiated simplicity is no longer the positive identity with itself the self–manifestation which is light as such, which constitutes the proper, inner self of the individual body; on the contrary, it is only a negative generality as the selfless moment of an other. This identity is therefore the seemingly harmless but insidious and consuming power of the individual and organic process. This element, air, behaves as a transparent but just as elastic fluid, which absorbs and penetrates everything.

§ 227.

(2) The elements of the antithesis are (a) being for itself not the indifferent being of rigidity, but rather being for itself posited in individuality as a moment, and therefore material selfhood, light identical to heat: fire. This element is materialised time, absolutely restless and consuming, and causes the self–consumption of the subsisting body as it conversely destroys the body through its external approach. In consuming another, fire consumes itself.

§ 228.

(b) The other element is the neutral element, the antithesis which coalesces into itself. Without individuality, however, and thus without rigidity and determination in itself it is a thoroughgoing equilibrium that dissolves all determinacy mechanically posited in it. It receives its limitation of shape only from outside, and without the unrest of the process in itself but at the most the possibility of process, namely, solubility. This element, water, can assume a gaseous and a solid form as a state apart from its characteristic state, that of internal indeterminacy.

§ 229.

(3) Earth, however, the element of the developed difference and its individual determination, is in the first place still indeterminate: earthiness, as such.

(c) The Elementary Process

§ 230.

The individual identity, by which the different elements in terms of both their difference from each other and their unity with each other are bound, is a dialectic which constitutes the physical life of the earth, the meteorological process. It is in this process alone that the elements, as dependent moments, have their existence, being generated in it and posited as existent.

just as the determinations of ordinary mechanics and the dependent bodies are applied to absolute mechanics and the free central bodies, so too, the finite physics of the single individual bodies is taken to be the same as the free, independent physics of the process of the earth. It is seen as a triumph of science that the same determinations are recognised and demonstrated in the general process of the earth as are found in the external and dependent processes of isolated physical corporeality. The demonstration of this likeness is effected by changing the determinations, through abstraction, from their characteristic differences and conditions into superficial generalities like attraction. Thus forces and laws are imaginatively drawn in which the particular, the concrete concept, and the conditions are lacking and are then fantasised as an addition, partly as an external substance and partly by analogy.

A primary difference marks the fixed idea 'of the substantial, immutable diversity of the elements, which is posited once and for all by the understanding on the basis of the processes of the isolated materials. Where higher transitions occur in these finite processes, where, for example, water is solidified into a crystal, where light and heat vanish, and so on, the obstinacy of formal thought has recourse to the nebulous and to some extent meaningless conceptions of 44 solution," "becoming bound or latent," and so on. Here, too, essentially belongs the transformation of all relationships in physical phenomena into "substances" and "materials," partly imponderable, so that each physical existence becomes the chaos previously mentioned of materials passing in and out of each other's pores. Such views conflict not only with every concept, but also with reasonable thinking.

§ 231.

The process of the earth is continuously ignited by its general self the activity of light, its primordial relationship to the sun. One moment of this process is the diremption of substantial identity, the development of moments of the independent antithesis into a tension between rigidity and selfless neutrality. Through this tension the earth tends towards resolution into, on the one hand, a crystal, a moon, or on the other hand into a fluid body, a comet, and the moments seek to realise their connection with their independent roots.

§ 232.

The other moment of the process is that being for itself towards which both sides of the antithesis strive, suspends itself as negativity pushed to its extreme;–it becomes the self–igniting destruction of the different existence sought by the moments. Through this process the substantial identity of the moments is produced, and the earth transforms itself into fertile individuality.

The thunderstorm is the complete manifestation of this process, whereas the other meteorological phenomena are beginnings or moments and undeveloped elaborations of it. Concerning thunderstorms, however, physics has so far been unable to propose a satisfactory explanation–since it limits its perspective to the conditions of the external process–, neither of rain formation (in spite of de Luc's observations and the conclusions drawn from them, and, among the Germans, the arguments made by the clever Lichtenberg against the theory of dissolution, whose conclusions have at least been retained to some extent) nor of lightning and thunder. It has had just as little success with other meteorological phenomena, in particular with meteorites, in which the process progresses as far as the beginning of an earthly core.

§ 233.

The concept of matter, gravity, sets out its moments in elemental nature, initially in the form of independent realities. The earth is initially the abstract ground of individuality, and posits itself in its process as the negative unity of the abstract, mutually separating elements, and consequently as the real ground and actuality of individualisation. Now, in this actuality, the elements present themselves as being unified together in concrete points of unity.

C. The Physics of Individuality

§ 234.

The individual body is matter, brought together by the particularity of the elements out of the generality of gravity and into individuality. Thus it is determined in and for itself and has by virtue of its individuality a characteristic form which constitutes the unity of the differentiation of a body. — This individuality is (a) immediate or at rest, a shape; (b) its separation into the diversity of features and the tension of differences; (c) process, in which the shape dissolves just as much as, in its determinateness in and for itself emerges.

(a) Shape

§ 235.

The individuality of matter in its immediate existence is the immanent form, which gives its own determinate difference to that material of the body which itself has in the first place only a superficial unit, and then one particular determinacy as its essence.

This is the shape, the specific kind of inward coherence of matter and its external border in space; — the individuality of the mechanism.

The specification of matter as an element is at this point shapeless, because it is still only a singularity. Regarding the form of the shape, and individuality in general, it is preferable to avoid the image of an external, mechanical style and composition. It may help in this case to distinguish between the externality of style and the inwardness of the shape's coherence, but the essential point is to remember the peculiar differentiation which arises from this distinction, which at the same time constitutes a determinate, self–identical unity in the relation.

§ 236.

The abstract specification is the specific gravity or density of matter, the relation of the weight of its mass to the volume. In this relation the material selfhood tears itself away from the abstract, general relations to the central body, ceases to be the uniform filling of space, and opposes a specific being in itself to an abstract being apart from itself

The varying density of matter is often explained by the assumption of pores; – though "to explain" means in general to refer a phenomenon back to the accepted, familiar determinations of the understanding, and no conceptions are more familiar than those of "composition," "pieces and their details," and "emptiness." Therefore nothing is clearer than to use the imaginative invention of pores to comprehend the densification of matter. These would be empty interstices, though physics does not demonstrate them, despite its attempt to speak of them as at hand and its claim to be based on experience and observation. What is beyond these and is merely assumed is the matter of thought. It does not occur to physics, however, that it has thoughts, which is true in at least two senses and here in a third sense: the pores are only imaginative inventions.

An immediate example of the peculiar specification of gravity offered by physics is furnished by the phenomenon that, when a bar of iron, evenly balanced on its fulcrum, is magnetised, it loses its equilibrium and shows itself to be heavier at one pole than at the other.–The axioms presupposed by physics in its mode of representing density are: (1) that equal amounts of equally large material parts weigh the same;–in this way the formal identity of gravity remains consistent–(2) the measure of the number of parts is the amount of weight, but (3) also of space, so that bodies of equal weight occupy equal amounts of space; (4) consequently, when equal weights are found in different volumes, the equality of the spaces is preserved by the assumption of pores which fill the space.

Kant has already contrasted intensity to the quantitative determination of the amount, and, instead of positing that the heavier body contains more particles in a certain space, he has assumed that in the heavier body the same number of particles fill space to a greater degree. In this way he created "dynamic physics." At least the determination of the intensive quantum would be just as correct as that of an extensive quantum; but this distinction (cf § 56) is empty and in itself nothing. Here the intensive determination of size, however, has this advantage: that it points to the category of measure and indicates initially a being in itself which as a conceptual determination is an immanent determinacy of form, and only existent as quantum. But to distinguish between extensive or intensive quantum differences, – and dynamic physics goes no further than this–does not express any reality.

§ 237.

Density is at first only a simple determinacy. The simple determinacy is, however, essentially a determination of form as a unity split apart from itself. Thus it constitutes the principle of brittleness, the shaping relation of its consistently maintained points.

The previously mentioned particles, molecules of matter, are an external determination of reflection. The real significance of the determination of the unit is that it is the immanent form of shaping.

§ 238.

The brittle is the subjective entity existing for itself but it must deploy the difference of the concept. The point becomes the line and posits itself as an opposed extreme to the line; the two are held by their middle term and point of indifference in their antithesis. This syllogism constitutes the principle of shaping in its developed determinacy, and is, in this abstract rigour, magnetism.

Magnetism is one of the determinations which inevitably became prominent when thought began to recognise itself in determinate nature and grasped the idea of a philosophy of nature. For the magnet exhibits in a simple, naive way the nature of the concept. The poles are not particular things; they do not possess sensory, mechanical reality, but rather an ideal reality; the point of indifference, in which they have their substance, is the unity in which they exist only as determinations of the concept, and the polarity is an opposition of only such moments. The phenomena revealed by magnetism as merely particular are merely and repeatedly the same determinations, and not diverse features which could add data to a description. That the individual magnetic needle points to the north, and thus to the south as well, is a manifestation of general terrestrial magnetism: in two such empirical magnets the poles named similarly repel each other, whereas the poles named differently attract. And precisely this is magnetism, namely, that the same or indifferent will split apart and oppose each other in the extreme, and the dissimilar or different will posit its indifference. The differently named poles have even been called friendly, and the similarly named poles have been called hostile.

The statement, however, that all bodies are magnetic has an unfortunate double meaning. The correct meaning is that all real, and not merely brittle, figures contain this concept; but the incorrect meaning is that all bodies also have this principle implicitly in its rigorous abstraction, as magnetism. It would be an unphilosophical thought to want to show that a form of the concept is at hand in nature, and that it exists universally in its determinacy as an abstraction. For nature is rather the idea in the element of being apart from itself so that, like the understanding, it retains the moments of the concept as dispersed and depicts them so in reality, but in the higher organic things the differentiated forms of the concept are unified as the highest concretion.

§ 239.

At the opposite end from magnetism, which as linear spatiality and the ideal contrast of extremes is the abstract concept of the shape, stands its abstract totality the sphere, the shape of the real absence of shape, of fluid indeterminacy, and of the indifferent elasticity of the parts.

§ 240.

Between the two actually shapeless extremes contained within magnetism as the abstract concept of the figure there appears, as an immanent form of juxtaposition distinct from that determined by gravity, a kind of magnetism transformed into total corporeality, cohesion.

§ 241.

The common understanding of cohesion merely refers to the individual moment of quantitative strength of the connection between the parts of a body. Concrete cohesion is the immanent form and determinacy of this connection, and comprehends both external crystallisations and the fragmentary shapes or central shapes, crystallisation which displays itself inwardly in transparent movement.

§ 242.

Through external crystallisation the individual body is sealed off as an individual against others, and capable of a mechanical process with them. As an inwardly formed entity the body specifies this process in terms of its behaviour as a merely general mass. In terms of its elasticity, hardness, softness, viscosity, and abilities to extend or to burst, the body retains its individual determinacy in resistance to external force.

§ 243.

As density, however, is at first only simple determinacy by virtue of the relation of volume to mass, cohesion is this simplicity as the selfhood of individuality. The self–preservation of the body during the vibration from a mechanical force is, therefore, also an emergence of its individual, pure ideality, its characteristic motion in itself through its whole cohesion. It is the specific determination of its ideal externality in itself through its self–identified time. In this vibration, the product of real force and external pressure which the body survives in the form of its specified ideality, this simple form achieves independent existence.

But entities without cohesion — which are inflexible and fluid are without resonance and in their resistance, which is merely an external vibration, make only a noise.

§ 244.

This individuality, since it is at first here only immediate, can be suspended by mechanical force. The friction, which brings together that difference of corporeality held apart by cohesion in the negativity of a temporal moment, causes an initial or concluding selfdestruction of the body to break forth. And the body exhibits its specific nature, in the relationship between the inner change and the suspension of its cohesion, through the capacity for heat.

(b) The Particularisation of Differences

§ 245.

Shaping, the individualisation of the mechanism or of weight, turns into elemental particularisation. The individual body has the totality of the elements within itself; as the subject of the same the body contains the elements in the first place as attributes or predicates, but in the second place these are retained only in immediate individuality, and thus they exist also as materials indifferent to each other. Thirdly, they are the relations to the unbound elements and the processes of the individual body with those elements.

In connection with the ancient, general idea that each body consists of the four elements, or with the more recent view of Paracelsus that it consists of mercury or liquid, sulphur or oil, and salt, and with many other ideas of this kind, it is to be remarked first that it is easy to refute these names if one understands by them only the particular empirical substances that they primarily denote. It is, however, not to be overlooked that these names were meant much more essentially to contain and to express the determinations of the concept. Thus we should rather wonder at the vehemence with which thought recognised only its own determination in such sensory things and held fast to its general significance. On the other hand, such a conception and determination, since it has reason as its source–which neither loses its way in the sensory games of phenomena and their confusion, nor allows itself to be brought to forget itself–is elevated infinitely far above the thoughtless investigation and chaotic narrative of the bodies' attributes. Here it is counted as a service and praiseworthy to have made yet another particular discovery, instead of referring the many particulars back to generality and the concept, and recognising the latter in them.

§ 246.

The body individualises: (a) the external self of light in its darkness into its specific opacity, colour; (b) air, as abstract, selfless generality into the simplicity of its specific process, or, as odour, is rather the specific individuality of the body in its simplicity, itself only as process; (c) water, the abstract neutrality, is individualised into the determinate neutrality of saltiness, acidity, and, immediately, into taste.

§ 247.

These particularised bodies are, in their general earthly totality, in the first place only superficially related to one another and preserve their independence by being isolated from each other. But as individuals they also stand in relation to each other and, to be sure, outside of the mechanical relationship as particular individualities.

§ 248.

At first these bodies relate to each other as independent entities, but they then become manifest as a mechanical relationship in an ideal movement, in the internal reverberation as sound. Now, however, in real selfhood, they emerge as an electrical relationship to each other.

§ 249.

The being for itself of these bodies, as it is manifested in physical contact, is posited in each by the difference from the other. Thus this being is not free, but rather an antithetical tension, in which, however, it is not the nature of the body which emerges: only the reality of its abstract self a light, is produced and, in fact, as a light set in opposition. The suspension of the diremption, the other moment of this process, has an undifferentiated light as its product, which disappears immediately as incorporeal. Apart from this abstract physical manifestation, the process has only the mechanical effect of shaking as a significant outcome.

It is well–known that the earlier distinction between vitreous and resinous electricity, determined as a part of sensory existence, was idealised by empirical science into the conceptual distinction between positive and negative electricity. This is a remarkable instance of the way in which empiricism, which initially attempts to grasp and retain generality in sensory form, suspends itself.

Although there has been much discussion recently of the polarisation of light, it would have been more appropriate to reserve this expression for electricity than for the phenomena observed by Malus, where transparent media, reflecting surfaces, and their various reciprocal inclinations, as well as a determinate corner of light, are actually so many different kinds of situations, which produces no difference in light itself but does show itself in light's shining.

The conditions under which positive and negative electricity emerge, in relation to smoother or rougher surfaces, for example, a breath of air, and so on, are proof of the superficiality of the electrical process, and show how little the concrete, physical nature of the body enters into it. Similarly, the weak coloration of the two electrical lights, and the smell and the taste of them, show only the beginning of a physicality in the abstract self of the light in which the process is maintained. Negativity, the suspension of the antithetical tension, is mainly a shock. The self–positing, self–identical self remains as such and consistent in the ideal spheres of space, time, and mechanism. Light has scarcely begun to materialise itself as warmth, and the combustion which can arise from the "discharge" is (Berthollet, Statique chimique, part I, sect. III, not. XI) rather a direct effect of shock than the consequences of the realisation of light as fire.

Galvanism is the electrical process made permanent; it is permanence as the contact between two different, non–brittle bodies, which, as part of their fluid nature (the "electrical conductive potential" of metal), their entire immediate difference towards each other, and the surface qualities of their relationship, maintain their tension mutually. The galvanic process occurs only through this particular specificity of bodies of a more concrete and corporeal nature, and subsequently undergoes a transition to the chemical process.

§ 250.

The individuality of the body is the negative unity of the concept, which is not self–positing simply as an immediate entity and an unmoved generality, but only in the mediation of the process. The body is therefore a product, and its shape a presupposition, for which the end that it will ultimately achieve is also presupposed. The particularisation of the body, however, does not stop at either mere inert diversity or the opposition between different attributes and their tension within the body's pure selfhood. Rather, since the particular attributes are only the reality of this simple concept, the body of their soul, of light, the entire corporeality moves into tension and the process which is the development of the individual body, a process of isolation; — the chemical process.

(c) The Process of Isolation

§ 251.

The chemical process has its products as a presupposition, and therefore begins (1) from the immediacy of their presupposition. In accord with the concept, the particular body is immediate insofar as its attributes or material components are unified together into a simple determination and become equal in the simplicity of specific gravity, thickness. Metals are solid, but in terms of their particularity become fluid and capable of maintaining a determinate difference towards each other.

§ 252.

The middle term, through which the concept with its reality unites these solid differences as the unity of both terms and the essence of each in itself, — posits the difference of one with the difference of the other into a unity, and therefore becomes real as the totality of their concept — is initially opposed to the immediate solidity of the extremes as an abstract neutrality, the element of water. The process itself is the decomposition of water into opposed moments through the presupposed difference of the extremes; they thereby suspend their abstraction and complete themselves as the unity of their concept.

§ 253.

The moments into which water decomposes or, what amounts to the same thing, the forms under which it is posited, are abstract, because water itself is only a physical element and not an individual physical body; — the chemical elements of the antithesis are oxygen and hydrogen. The metals, however, which have been integrated in the process, also receive only an abstract integration from that abstract middle term, a reality which is only a positing of their difference, an oxide.

The condition of lime as an oxide lies closest to the condition of metals, due to the inner indifference of their solid nature. But nature's inability to hold on to the specific concept also allows individual metals to change so far in the opposite direction that their oxide immediately comes to resemble acids. It is well known that chemistry can portray, as amalgamations at least, the metallic components of lime and potash, but also ammonia, strontium, barytes, and indeed, even of different soils, and thereby depict these bodies as oxides. To be sure, the chemical elements are such abstractions that when they are in the form of gases, in which they become manifest for themselves, they interpenetrate like light and, notwithstanding their ponderability, their materiality and impenetrability reveal themselves here to be raised to immateriality. Furthermore, oxygen and hydrogen have a determination so dependent upon the individuality of the body that the components of oxygen are determined in oxides, as a base in general, and, in the opposite direction, as an acid, just as, by contrast, the acidic determination in hydrochloric acid reveals itself as hydrogenation.

§ 254.

In contrast to the solid indifference of the particular corporeality stands physical brittleness, the being of particularity grasped together in the unity of selfhood (brass represents the totality, as the unification of sulphur and metal). This brittleness is the real possibility of combustion, the reality of which is itself the self–devouring being for itself fire, and remains an external entity. Fire mediates the inner difference of the combustible body through the physical element of abstract negativity, air, with a being as posited or reality, and enhances it to acidity. Air, however, decomposes in its negative principle into this, oxygen, and a dead positive residuum, nitrogen.

§ 255.

The chemical elements are: nitrogen, the abstraction of indifference; oxygen, the element of self–subsistent difference, the burning element; hydrogen, the element belonging to the opposition or self–subsistent indifference, the combustible element; and carbon, as the abstraction of their individual element.

§ 256.

(2) The two products of the abstract processes, acids and bases or alkalis, are now no longer merely but actually diverse, and (concentrated acids and alkalis enhanced caustically) are therefore incapable of subsisting for themselves. In a state of restlessness they suspend themselves, and are posited as identical to their opposites. This unity, in which their concept is realised, is the neutral body, salt.

§ 257.

(3) In salt the concrete and shaped body is the product of its process. The relation of such diverse bodies to each other involves to some extent the more precise particularisation of the bodies, from which "elective affinities" derive. In general, however, these processes are for themselves more real, since the extremes occurring in them are not abstract bodies. More specifically, they are the dissolved particles of the neutral bodies into abstractions, the processes from which they are produced, retrogressions back to oxides and acids, and further, both immediately and in abstract forms, back to the indifferent bases, which manifest themselves in this way as products.

Empirical chemistry deals mainly with the particularity of the products, which are then ordered according to superficial and abstract determinations. Metals, oxygen nitrogen and many other bodies, earth, sulphur, phosphorous appear in this order together; just as chaotically, the more abstract and the more real processes are posited on the same level. If a scientific form is to come from this mixture, then each product should be determined according to the level of the process from which it results and which gives it its particular significance. It is just as essential to distinguish the levels of the abstraction or the reality of the process. Animal and vegetable substances belong in any case to an entirely different order, and so little of their nature can be comprehended through the description of the chemical process that much more is destroyed than saved, and only the course of its death is grasped. These substances, however, should serve to work against that metaphysics dominant in both chemistry and physics, namely, the thought or empty idea of the unchangeability of matter, its composition and subsistence in matter. We see admitted in general, however, that chemical substances lose those attributes in combination which they demonstrate separately. Nevertheless the idea remains that these substances are the same things with the attributes as without, and as things with these attributes they are not only products of the process.

An important step towards simplification of the particularities in the elective affinities is the law discovered by Richter and Guiton Morveau, which states that neutral compounds suffer no change regarding their state of solution when they are mixed in solution and the acids exchange bases with each other. The quantitative scale of acids and alkalis has been constructed on the basis of this law, according to which each individual acid has a particular relation for its saturation to each alkali; so that, however, for every other acid whose quantitative unity is only different from the others, now the alkalis have among each other the same relation to their saturation as to the other acids, and similarly, acids display a constant relation among each other and relative to all the different alkali.

Since, moreover, the chemical process has its determination in the concept, the empirical conditions of a particular form, as for example electricity, are not as fixed as sensory determinations and not as abstract moments as is represented for example by an elective affinity. Berthollet, in his famous work Statique chimique, has brought together and investigated the circumstances which produce changes in the results of chemical action, results often attributed only to the conditions of the affinity, which are taken as constant and fixedly determined laws. He says: "The superficiality which these explanations bring into science is prominently regarded as progress."

§ 258.

The chemical process is, to be sure, in general terms, life, for the individual body in its immediacy is suspended and brought forth by the process, so that the concept no longer remains an inner necessity, but becomes manifest. But the body also achieves a mere appearance, and not objectivity. This process is finite and transient, because the individual body has immediate individuality, and therefore a limited particularity, so that the process has immediate and contingent conditions. Fire and differentiation are extinguished in the neutral body, and it does not break apart sufficiently in itself to divide. Similarly, difference exists at first in indifferent independence, but does not stand for itself in relation to the other, nor does it activate itself

Certain chemical phenomena have led chemists to apply the determination of purposiveness in explaining them. An example is the f that an oxide is reduced to a lower degree of oxidation than that at which it can combine with the acid working on it, and a part of it is more strongly oxidised–,–here the self–determination of the concept lies in the realisation.

§ 259.

In the chemical process the body thus displays the transiency of its immediate individuality both in its emergence and its passing away, and presents itself as a moment of generality. In this immediate individuality the concept has the reality which corresponds to it, a concrete generality which derives from particularisation, and at the same time contains in itself the conditions and moments of the total syllogism which fall apart from each other in the immediate chemical process; — the organism.

III. Organic Physics

A. Geological Nature – B. Vegetable Nature – C. The Animal Organism

§ 260.

The real totality of the individual body, in which its particularity is made into a product and equally suspends itself — elevates itself in the process into the first ideality of nature, but an ideality which is fulfilled, and as self–related negative unity has essentially attained selfhood and become subjective. With this accomplished, the idea has entered into existence, initially as an immediate existence, Life. This is: (a) as shape, the general image of life, the geological organism; (b) as particular or formal subjectivity, vegetable nature; (c) as individual, concrete subjectivity, animal nature.

A. Geological Nature

§ 261.

The general system of individual bodies is the earth, which in the chemical process initially has its abstract individuality in particularisation, but as the totality it has an infinite relation to itself as a general, self–dividing process; – and is, immediately, the subject and its product. As the immediate totality, however, presupposed by subjective totality itself the body of the earth is only the shape of the organism.

§ 262.

The members of this organism do not contain, therefore, the generality of the process within themselves, they are the particular individuals, and constitute a system whose forms manifest themselves as members of the unfolding of an underlying idea, whose process of development is a past one.

§ 263.

The powers of this process, which nature leaves behind as independent entities beyond earth, are the connection and the position of the earth in the solar system, its solar, lunar, and cometary life, the inclination of its axis to the orbit and the magnetic axis. Standing in closer relation to these axes and their polarisation is the distribution of sea and land: the compact spreading of land in the north, the division and sharp tapering of the parts towards the south, the further separation into an old and a new world, and the further division of the former into continents distinguished from one another and from the new world by their physical, organic, and anthropological character, to which an even younger and more immature continent is joined; — mountain ranges, and so on.

§ 264.

The physical organisation of the earth shows a series of stages of granitic activity, involving a core of mountains in which the trinity of determinations is displayed, and leads through other forms which are partly transitions and modifications, though its totality remains the existing foundation, only more unequal and unformed within itself This is partly also an elaboration of its moments into a more determinate difference and more abstract mineral moments, such as metals and fossil objects generally, until it loses itself in mechanical stratifications and alluvial terrains lacking any immanent formative development.

§ 265.

This crystal of life, the inanimate organism of the earth which has its concept in the sidereal connection but possesses its own process as a presupposed past, is the immediate subject of the meteorological process, which as an organised whole is in its complete determinateness. In this objective subject the formerly elementary process is now objective and individual, — the suspension of immediacy takes place, through which general individuality now emerges for itself and life becomes vital or real. The first real vitality, which the fructified earth brings forth, is vegetable nature.

B. Vegetable Nature

§ 266.

The generality and individuality of life are still immediately identical in immediate vitality. Consequently the process by which the plant differentiates itself into distinct parts and sustains itself is one in which it comes out of itself and falls into pieces as several individuals, for which the whole plant is more the basis than a subjective unity. A further consequence is that the differentiation of the organic parts is only a superficial metamorphosis, and one part can easily pass into the function of the other.

§ 267.

The process of shaping and reproduction of the single individual coincides in this way with the process of genus formation. And because self–like generality, the subjective unit of individuality, does not separate itself from real particularisation but is only submerged in it, the plant does not move from its place, nor is it a selfinterrupting individualisation, but a continually flowing self–nourishment. It does not relate itself to individualised inorganic nature, but to the general elements. Nor is it capable of feeling and animal warmth.

§ 268.

Insofar, however, as life is essentially the concept which realises itself only through self–division and reunification, the plant processes also diverge from each other. (1) But their inner process of formation is to be seen partly as the positive, merely immediate transformation of nourishment supplies into the specific nature of plants. On the one hand, and for the sake of essential simplicity, this is the division into abstract generality of an implicitly inseparable individuality, as into the negative of vitality, becoming wood. But on the other hand, on the side of individuality and vitality, this is the process specifying itself in an outward direction.

§ 269.

(2) This is the unfolding of the parts as organs of different elementary relations, the division partly into the relation to earth and into the air and water process which mediates them. Since the plant does not hold itself back in inner, subjective generality against outer individuality, it is equally torn out of itself by light, from which it takes the specific confirmation and individualisation of itself knotted and multiplied into a multiplicity of individuals.

§ 270.

Since, however, the reproduction of the individual vegetable as a singularity is not the subjective return into itself a feeling of self but inwardly becomes wooden, the production of the self of the plant consequently moves in an outward direction. The plant brings forth its light as its own self in the blossom, in which the neutral colour green is determined as a specific coloration, or, too, light is produced as a white colour, purified from the dark.

§ 271.

Since the plant in this way offers itself as a sacrifice, this exteriorisation is at the same time the concept realised by the process, the plant, which has produced itself as a whole, but which in the process has come into opposition with itself. This, the highest point of the process, is therefore the beginning of the process of sexual differentiation which occurs in the process of genus formation.

§ 272.

(3) The process of genus formation, as distinct from the processes of formation and reproduction of the individual, is an excess in the actuality of plant nature, because those processes also directly involve a dissolution into many individuals. But in the concept the process is, like subjectivity which has converged with itself that generality in which the

plant suspends the immediate individuality of its organic life, and thereby grounds the transition into the higher organism.

C. The Animal Organism

§ 273.

Organic individuality exists as subjectivity insofar as its individuality is not merely immediate actuality but also and to the same extent suspended, exists as a concrete moment of generality, and in its outward process the organism inwardly preserves the unity of the self This is the nature of the animal which, in the reality and externality of individuality, is equally, by contrast, immediately and inwardly self–reflected individuality, inwardly existing subjective generality.

§ 274.

The animal has contingent self–movement because its subjectivity is, like light and fire, ideality torn from gravity, — a free time, which, as removed at the same time from real externality, determines its place on the basis of inner chance. Bound up with this is the animal's possession of a voice in which its subjectivity, existing in and for itself dominates the abstract ideality of time and space, and manifests its self–movement as a free vibration within itself. It has animal warmth, as a permanent preservation of the shape; interrupted intussusception; but primarily feeling, as the individuality which in its determinacy is immediately general for itself and really selfdifferentiating individuality.

§ 275.

The animal organism, as living generality, is the concept which passes through its three determinations, each of which is in itself the same total identity of substantial unity and, at the same time and as determined for itself by the form, is the transition into others, so that the totality results from this process. It is only as this selfreproducing entity, not as an existing one, that the animal organism is living.

§ 276.

The animal organism is therefore: (a) a simple, general being in itself in its externality, whereby real determinacy is immediately taken up as particularity into the general, and is thereby the unseparated identity of the subject with itself; — sensibility; — (b) particularity, as excitability from the outside and, on the other hand, the counter–effect coming from the outward movement of the subject; — irritability; — (c) the unity of these moments, the negative return to itself through the relation of externality, and thereby the generation and positing of itself as an individual; — reproduction. Inwardly, this is the reality and foundation of the first moments, and outwardly, this is the articulation of the organism and its armament.

§ 277.

These three moments of the concept have their reality in three systems, namely, the nervous system, the circulatory system, and the digestive system. The first is in the systems of the bones and sensory apparatus, whereas the second turns outwardly on two sides in the lungs and the muscles. The digestive system is, however, as a system of glands with skin and cellular tissue, immediate, vegetative, reproductive, but as part of the actual system of the intestines it is the mediating reproduction. The animal thus divides itself in the center (insectum) into three systems, the head, thorax, and the abdomen, though, on the other hand, the extremities used for mechanical movement and grasping constitute the moment of the individuality outwardly positing and differentiating itself.

§ 278.

The idea of the living organism is the manifested unity of the concept with its reality; as the antithesis of that subjectivity and objectivity, however, this unity exists essentially only as process. It exists at the same time as the movement of the abstract relation of the living entity to itself which dissolves itself into particularity, and, as the return into itself it is the negative unity of subjectivity and totality. Each of these moments is itself a process, however as a concrete moment of the living, and the whole is the unity of the three processes.

§ 279.

(1) The abstract process of living individuality is the process of inner formation in which the organism converts its own members into a inorganic nature, into means, and feeds on itself Thus it produces precisely this totality of its self–organisation, so that each member is reciprocally the end and the means, and maintains itself through the others and in opposition to them. It is the process which has the simple feeling of self as a result.

§ 280.

(2) The self–feeling of individuality is, in its negative return into itself immediately exclusive and in a state of tension with inorganic nature as with real and external nature. (3) Since animal organisation is immediately reflected into itself in this external relation, this ideal relationship is the theoretical process and, indeed, the determinate feeling, which differentiates itself into the multiple sensory qualities of inorganic nature.

§ 281.

The senses and the theoretical processes are therefore: (1) the sense of the mechanical sphere of gravity, of cohesion and its variation, of heat, and feeling as such; (2) the senses of antithesis, of the particularised principle of air, and of equally realised neutrality, of water, and of the antitheses of its dissolution; — smell and taste; (3) the sense of the pure, essential, but exterior identity, of the side belonging to the materials of gravity: fire, light, and colour; and (4) the sense for the depiction of subjective reality, or of the independent inner ideality of the body standing in opposition, the sense of hearing.

The threefold moments of the concept therefore convert here into a fivefold number, because the moment of particularity or of the antithesis in its totality is itself threefold. Another reason for the transition is that the animal organism is the reduction of inorganic nature split apart from itself but at the same time it is its developed totality. Because it is still natural subjectivity, the moments of nature's developed totality exist separately, but as an infinite unity. The determinations of this subjectivity, therefore, have the sense of touch as their particular sense, the most fundamental, general sense, which thus could also better be called feeling. Particularity is the antithesis, and this is the identity and the antithesis itself Thus the sense of light belongs to this particularity, an identity which constitutes one side of the antithesis, as abstract, but precisely therefore determines itself. Also belonging here are the two senses of the antithesis itself as such, air and water, both like the others in their embodied specification and individualisation. To the sense of individuality belongs that subjectivity which, as purely self–demonstrating subjectivity, is tone.

§ 282.

The real process of inorganic nature begins equally with feeling, namely, the feeling of real externality, and with this feeling the negation of the subject, which is at the same time the positive relation to itself and its certainty in contrast to its negation. It begins with the feeling of a lack, and the drive to suspend the lack, which is the condition of being stimulated externally.

Only what is living feels a lack, for it alone in nature is the concept, the unity of itself and of its specific opposite; in this relation it is a subject. Where there is a limitation, it is a negation only for a third, an external reflection. It is lack, however, insofar as in one sense the overcoming of the lack is also at hand, and the contradiction is posited as such. A being which is capable of having and enduring the contradiction of itself in itself is the subject; this constitutes its finitude. — Reason proves its infinitude precisely at that point when reference is made to finite reason, since it determines itself as finite. For negation is finitude and a lack only for that which is the suspended being of itself the infinite relation to itself. Thoughtlessness, however, stops short at the abstraction of the limitation, and in life, too, where the concept itself enters into existence, it fails to grasp the concept, but remains fixed on the determinations of representation: drives, instincts, and needs.

An important step towards a true representation of the organism is the substitution of the category of stimulation by external forces for the category of the intervention of external causes. This latter contains the beginning of idealism, the assertion that nothing at all can have a positive relation to the living if the living being is not in and for itself the possibility of the relation itself that is, not determined by the concept, and thus in general not immanent to the subject.

But perhaps the most unphilosophical of any such scientific concoctions of the reflective categories is the introduction of such formal and material relationships into the theory of stimulation, which has long been regarded as philosophical. This includes for example the entirely abstract antithesis of receptivity to active capacity, which supposedly stand to each other as factors in inverse relations of magnitude. The result of this is to reduce all differences in the organism to the formalism of a merely quantitative differentiation, involving increase and decrease, strengthening and weakening, in other words, removing all possible traces of the concept. A theory of medicine built on these and determinations of the understanding is complete in half a dozen propositions, and it is no wonder that it spread rapidly and found many adherents.

The cause of this philosophical confusion, which initiated the tendency to befriend nature, lay in the basic error of initially determining the absolute as the absolute indifference of subject and object, and then treating all determinations as only quantitative differences. It is the case, rather, that the absolute form, the concept and the principle of life, has for its soul only the qualitative difference which consumes itself in itself But because this truly infinite negativity was not recognised, it was believed that the absolute identity of life, as the attributes and the modes in the external understanding are for Spinoza, can not be fixed without making the difference into a merely external difference of the reflection. In this way, however, life is left altogether lacking the salient point of selfhood, the principle of self–movement, the differentiation of the self and the principle of individuality in general.

Another crude and utterly unphilosophical procedure is the one which attempted to give the formal determinations a real meaning by replacing the conceptual determinations with carbon and nitrogen, oxygen and hydrogen, and determined the difference previously characterised as intensive as now more or less of the one or another substance, whereas the active and positive relation of the external stimulus would be the addition of a lacking substance. One example is the assertion that in an asthenia, or a nerve fever, nitrogen has the upper hand in the organism because the brain and nerves are supposedly in general intensified nitrogen, since chemical analysis has shown this to be the principal ingredient of these organic structures. The ingestion of carbon is therefore supposedly indicated in order to restore the balance of these substances, in other words, in order to restore health. The remedies which have been shown to work empirically against nerve fever are, for this same reason, regarded as belonging to the side of carbon, and this superficial compilation and opinion are presented as explanation and proof The crudity of this procedure consists in taking the external Caput mortuum, the dead substance, a dead life which chemistry has already destroyed a second time, for the essence of a living organ, and indeed, for its concept.

This last argument gives rise to that highly facile formalism which replaces the determinations of the concept with sensuous materials like chemical substances, as well as relationships belonging to the sphere of inorganic nature, like the north and south polarity of magnetism, or the differences between magnetism and electricity. This is a formalism which conceives the natural universe and develops its conception in such a way that it attaches a readymade schema of north and south or east and west polarities externally to the spheres and differences it uses. For this purpose there is a great variety of forms possible. For it remains a matter of choice whether one employs the determinations of the totality for the schema, as they appear for example in the chemical sphere, oxygen, hydrogen, and so on, and transfers them to magnetism, mechanism, electricity, and the masculine and the feminine, contraction and expansion, and so on, then applies them to the other spheres.

§ 283.

Need and excitement are connected to the relation between the universal and the particular mechanism (sleeping and waking), the relation to air (breathing and skin processes), water (thirst), and the individualised earth, namely, the particular forms of the earth (cf. hunger, § 275). Life, the subject of these moments of totality, develops inwardly a tension between itself as concept and the moments of a reality external to itself and is the ongoing conflict in which it overcomes this externality. Because the animal can only exist as an essentially individual entity, and this only individually, this objectification is not adequate to its concept and therefore turns back constantly from its satisfaction to the condition of need.

§ 284.

The mechanical seizure of the external object is only the beginning of the unification of the object with the living animal. Since the animal is hence a subject, the simple negativity of the punctured unity, the assimilation can be neither of a mechanical nor a chemical nature, for in these processes both the material substances as the conditions and the activity remain externally in opposition to each other, and lack living, absolute unity.

§ 285.

In the first place, because the living organism is the general power over the nature external and opposed to it, assimilation is the immediate fusion of the ingested material with animality, an infection by the latter and simple transformation (cf. § 278). Secondly, since the power of the living organism is the relation of itself to itself in mediation, assimilation is digestion. It is the opposition of the subject to its immediate assimilation, so that the former stimulates itself on the other hand as a negative, and emerges as the process of the antithesis, the process of animal water (of stomach and pancreatic juices, animal lymph as such) and of animal fire (of the gall, in which the accomplished return of the organism into itself from its concentration in the spleen is determined as being for itself as active consumption).

§ 286.

This animal stimulation is turned at first against the external potency, which, however, is placed immediately on the side of the organism by the infection (§ 277). But this stimulus, as the antithesis and the being for itself of the process, has at the same time the determination of externality over against the generality and simple self–relation of the living organism. Both aspects together, initially appearing on the side of the subject as means, actually constitute therefore the object and the negative side in conflict with the organism, which has to overcome and to digest.

§ 287.

This inversion of attitude is the reflection of the organism into itself the negation of its own negativity of outwardly directed activity. As a natural being it combines the individuality which it reaches in the process with its generality as disjunctive, in such a way that on the one hand it separates from itself the first negation, the externality of the object and its own activity, on the other hand, and as immediately identical with this negation, with this means reproduces itself Thus the outward moving process is transformed and transposed into the first formal processes of reproduction from its own self.

The primary moment in digestion is the immediate action of life as the power over the inorganic object, which it sets against itself and presupposes as its stimulating attraction only insofar as it is itself identical with it. This action is infection and immediate transformation. It has been empirically demonstrated and shown to accord with the concept, by the experiments of Spallanzani and others and by recent physiology, that this immediacy, which the living organism has as a generality, continues itself into its food without any further mediation, by its mere contact with it and simply by taking it up into its own warmth and sphere. This is a refutation of both the theory of a mechanical, fictitious sorting out and separating of parts already homogeneous and useful, and the theory of mediation conceived as a chemical process. But the investigations of the mediating actions have not found more specific moments in this transformation (as appears, for example, in vegetable substances as a series of fermentations). On the contrary, they have shown for cxample that a great deal of food moves straight from the stomach into the mass of gastric juices, without passing through other mediating stages, that the pancreatic juice is further nothing more than saliva, that the pancreas could quite as well be dispensed with, and so on.

The last product, the chyle, which the thoracic duct takes up and which is discharged into the blood, is the same lymph which is secreted by each intestine and organ, effects the skin and lymphatic system in the immediate process of transformation, and is everywhere found already prepared. The lower organisms of animal life, which, moreover, are nothing more than lymph coagulated into a membranous point or tube — a simple intestinal canal — do not go beyond this immediate transformation. The mediated digestive process in the higher organisations of animal life is, in respect of its characteristic product, just such a superfluity as, in the plant, the generation of seeds mediated by "sexual difference." The faeces often show, especially in children, in whom after all the increase of material is most apparent, the greatest part of the food unchanged, mixed mainly with animal substances, bile, phosphorus, and the like, and the primary action of the organism to be to overcome and to eliminate its own products.

The syllogism of the organism is not, therefore, the syllogism of external purposiveness, for it does not stop at directing its activity and form against the outer subject but makes this process, which because of its externality is on the verge of becoming mechanical and chemical, into an object itself And since it is nature, in the uniting of itself with itself in its outward process, it is no less a disjunctive activity, which rids itself of this process, abstracts itself away from its anger towards the object, from this one–sided subjectivity, and thereby becomes for itself what it is in itself: the identity of its concept and its reality. Thus the end and the product of its activity are found to be that which it already is originally and at the beginning. In this way the satisfaction accords with reason: the process outward into external differentiation is converted into the process of the organism with itself and the result is not the mere production of a means, but of the end.

§ 288.

Through the process with external nature the animal achieves self–certainty and its subjective concept, truth and objectivity as a single individual. And it is the production of itself just as much as its self–preservation, or reproduction as production of its first concept. Thus the concept joins together with itself and is, as concrete generality, genus. The disjunction of the individual finding itself in the genus is the sexual difference, the relation of the subject to an object which is itself such a subject.

§ 289.

This relation is the drive: the individual as such is not adequate to its genus, nor does this adequacy fall into an external reflection. The individual is at the same time, in this limitation of the genus, the identical relation of the genus to itself in one unity. The individual thus has the feeling of this lack and exists in the natural difference of the sexes.

§ 290.

(3) The process of genus formation has, as in the inorganic process of chemism, taken the general concept as the essence of individuals to a general extreme. The tension between the individual and the inadequacy of its single actuality drives each to have its self–feeling only in the other of its genus, and to integrate itself through union with the other. Through this mediation the concrete generality joins together with itself and yields individual reality.

§ 291.

This product is the negative identity of the differentiated individuals and is, as realised genus, an asexual life. But on the side of nature the product is only implicitly this genus and distinct from the individuals which have perished in it. It is thus itself an individual which has in itself the determination of the same difference and transiency. But at the same time, in this new life in which individuality is suspended, the same subjectivity is retained positively and in this, its return into itself the genus as such has emerged for itself in reality, and has become a higher being than nature.

§ 292.

Underlying the various orders and structures of the animals lies the general type of the animal determined by the concept, which nature manifests partly in the different steps of its development from the simplest organisation to the most complete, in which it is the instrument of the spirit, and partly in the different circumstances and conditions of elementary nature.

The concept of the animal has the concept itself as its essence, because it is the actuality of the idea of life. The nature of its generality enables it to have a simpler and more developed existence which corresponds more or less to it. Thus the concept in its determinacy can not be grasped from existence itself. The classes, in which it emerges developed and manifested completely in its moments, appear as a particular existence in contrast to the others, and can also have a bad existence in them. The concept is already presupposed for the judgment of whether the existence is bad. If, as usual, existence is presupposed, then it will undoubtedly be used in an empirical way to reach no fixed determination, and all particular attributes will also seem to be lacking. Acephalous animals, for example, have been used as proof that people can live without brains.

Zoology, like the natural sciences generally, has concerned itself primarily with discovering more certain and simpler signs for subjective cognition. Only since this goal of an "artificial" system for classifying animals was given up has the way been opened for a broader view, and among the empirical sciences there is hardly one which in recent times has expanded as much as zoology, particularly through its auxiliary science of comparative anatomy. This expansion has not occurred solely in the sense of more observations, for none of the sciences lacks these, but in the sense of arranging its material to accord with reason.

Partly it is the habits of individual animals, viewed as a coherent whole determining the construction of every part, which have become the main point, so that the great founder of comparative anatomy, Cuvier, could boast that he could recognise the essential nature of the entire animal from a single bone. Partly it is that the general type of the animal has been traced in the various, still apparently incomplete and disparate forms, and its importance recognised in the hardly noticed suggestion, as well as in the mixture of organs and functions, and in this way has been raised above and beyond its particularity into its generality. A primary feature of this method is the recognition of how nature shapes and adapts this organism to the particular element in which it is placed, an environment which can also be one particular species of plant or another of animal. It is due to the immediacy of the idea of life that the concept, whether or not it is only determined in and for itself does not exist as such in life. Its existence is therefore subjected to the manifold conditions and circumstances of external nature, and can appear in the most inadequate forms. The fecundity of the earth causes life to break out in every way. Even perhaps less than the other spheres of nature, therefore, can the animal world present in itself an independent, rational system of organisation, or retain a hold on forms determined by the concept and preserve them against the imperfection and mixture of conditions, from confusion, degeneration, and transitional forms. This weakness of the concept, which exists in the animal though not in its fixed, independent freedom, entirely subjects even the genus to the changes that are shared by the life of the animal. And the environment of external contingency in which the animal must live exercises perpetual violence against the individual. Hence the life of the animal seems in general to be sick, and the animal's feeling seems to be insecure, anxious, and unhappy.

§ 293.

Due to the externality of its existence, the individual organism can not accord with its determination. It finds itself in a state of disease when one of its systems or organs, stimulated to conflict with an organic power, establishes itself for itself and persists in its particular activity against the activity of the whole. For the fluidity and pervasive process of the activity is thus obstructed.

§ 294.

The characteristic manifestation of disease is, thus, when the identity of the entire organic concept, as the successive course of life's movement through its different moments, sensibility, irritability, and reproduction, presents itself as fever. This fever is to the same extent both the isolated activity in opposition to the course of totality, and the effort towards and beginning of healing.

§ 295.

Medicine provokes the organism to remove the inorganic power with which the activity of the individual organ or system is entangled and thereby isolated. Essentially, however, the irritation of the formal activity of the particular organ or system is suspended, and its fluidity is restored within the whole. The medicine achieves this as an irritant, but one which is even more difficult to assimilate and to overcome, and against which the organism is compelled to exert its entire strength. While it acts in this way against an external entity, the organism steps out of the limitation with which it had become identical and in which it had become involved.

Medication must in general be viewed as an indigestible substance. But indigestibility is only a relative category, though not in the vague sense in which it is usually taken, as if it really meant something easily digestible by weaker constitutions. On the contrary, such an easily digestible substance is indigestible for stronger individuals. The true relativity, that of the concept, which has its actuality in life, consists, when expressed in the quantitative terms which count as valid here, in homogeneity being greater, the more the opposed terms are intrinsically self–subsistent. The highest qualitative form of relativity in the living organism has manifested itself as the sexual relation, in which independent individualities are identical to each other.

For the lower forms of animal life, which have not achieved a difference within themselves, the digestible substance is the substance without individuality, such as water for plants. For children, the digestible substance is partly the completely homogeneous animal lymph, mother's milk, a substance which is already digested or rather has further differentiated within itself and partly the least individualised of mixed substances. Substances of this kind, on the other hand, are indigestible for stronger natures. These natures digest more easily individualised animal substances, or plant juices which sunlight has matured to a more powerful self and are therefore "spirituous," instead of for example, the vegetable products still in their merely neutral colour and closer to the chemical process proper. Through this more intensive selfhood the former substances form an even stronger contrast, but for that very reason they are more homogeneous irritants. Taken together, medications are negative irritants, poisons, a stimulant and at the same time an indigestible substance, to the extent that the organism alienated from itself in disease must gather up its strength, turn against the medication as an external, foreign body, and thereby achieve again the self–feeling of its individuality.

But Brownianism, regarded as a complete system of medicine, is merely an empty formalism, especially in its determination of diseases and the actions of medications according to sthenic or asthenic body types, the latter further divided into direct and indirect asthenia. Brown's theory is, moreover, too often limited by formulations derived from the natural sciences, such as his recourse to the factors of carbon and nitrogen, oxygen and hydrogen as explanations, or magnetic, electrical, and chemical moments. Nevertheless, his theory did have two important consequences: through him, the view of merely particular and specific issues, both in diseases and medications, was expanded to the general in them as essential elements; and through his opposition to the previously used method, which was even more fixed on asthenic and asthenising questions than the subsequent phases, he showed that the organism does not react to the most antithetical kind of treatment in such an opposite way, but that frequently, at least in the final results, it reacts in a similar and hence general way. Thus the simple identity of the organism with itself as its true essence is demonstrated in opposition to a particular entanglement of one of its systems with specific irritants.

§ 296.

The animal individual, in overcoming and moving beyond particular inadequacies in conflict with its concept, does not suspend the inadequacy in general which it has within it, namely, that its idea is the immediate idea, or that the animal stands within nature. Its subjectivity is only the concept in itself but not itself for itself and exists only as an immediate individuality. That inner generality is thus opposed to its actuality as a negative power, from which the animal suffers violence and perishes, because its existence does not itself contain this generality within itself.

§ 297.

As abstract, this negative generality is an external actuality which exerts mechanical violence against the animal and destroys it. As its own concrete generality it is the genus, and the living organism submerges its different individuality partly in the process of genus formation. Partly, however, the living organism directly suspends its inadequacy in relation to the genus, which is its original sickness and the inborn seed of death, since it imagines the individuality of its death. But because this generality is immediate, the individual achieves only an abstract objectivity, it blunts its activity, grows ossified, and thus kills itself by itself.

§ 298.

But the subjectivity of the living organism is just as essentially in itself identical to concrete generality and the genus. Its identity with the genus is thus only the suspension of the formal antithesis, of immediacy, and of the generality of individuality. Since this subjectivity is, moreover, the concept in the idea of life, it is in itself the absolute being in itself of reality. Through this suspension of its immediacy subjectivity coalesces itself absolutely with itself and the last self–externality of nature is suspended. In this way nature has passed over into its truth, into the subjectivity of the concept, whose objectivity is itself the suspended immediacy of individuality, the concrete generality, the concept which has the concept as its existence — into the spirit.

Printed in the United Kingdom
by Lightning Source UK Ltd.
108841UKS00002B/26

9 781419 177224